THE PRIMITIVE OBSERVATORY

Crab Orchard Series in Poetry
First Book Award

THE PRIMITIVE OBSERVATORY

POEMS BY GREGORY KIMBRELL

Crab Orchard Review & Southern Illinois University Press

Carbondale

Southern Illinois University Press
www.siupress.com

19 18 17 16   4 3 2 1

The Crab Orchard Series in Poetry is a joint publishing venture
of Southern Illinois University Press and *Crab Orchard Review*. This
series has been made possible by the generous support of the Office
of the President of Southern Illinois University and the Office of
the Vice Chancellor for Academic Affairs and Provost at Southern
Illinois University Carbondale.

Editor of the Crab Orchard Series in Poetry: Jon Tribble
Judge for the 2014 First Book Award: Brian Barker

Cover illustration: "Demolition of Old Station Tower," 1914, Santa Fe
Railroad Station, San Diego, California. Library of Congress, Prints
and Photographs Online Catalog.

Library of Congress Cataloging-in-Publication Data
Kimbrell, Gregory.
[Poems. Selections]
The primitive observatory : poems / by Gregory Kimbrell.
  pages cm. — (Crab orchard series in poetry)
ISBN 978-0-8093-3480-3 (pbk. : alk. paper)
ISBN 978-0-8093-3481-0 (e-book)
I. Title.
PS3611.I4583A6 2016
811'.6—dc23   2015031729

Printed on recycled paper. ♻

The paper used in this publication meets the minimum
requirements of American National Standard for Information
Sciences—Permanence of Paper for Printed Library Materials,
ANSI Z39.48-1992. ∞

CONTENTS

ACKNOWLEDGMENTS

I thank, first of all, my poetry teachers Carol Ann Davis, Gregory Donovan, Claudia Emerson, Kathleen Graber, Elizabeth Seydel Morgan, and David Wojahn, because this book would not exist without their guidance. I also thank my fellow students from the MFA in Creative Writing Program at Virginia Commonwealth University for their critiques of early versions of many of the poems collected here. Several friends took the time to read drafts of the completed book and share their thoughts: Meriah Crawford, J. T. Glover, Lea Marshall, Bri Spicer, and Patrick Scott Vickers. And Emilia Phillips encouraged—and humored—me during every stage of preparing this book.

Many thanks to Jon Tribble, Allison Joseph, the staffs of *Crab Orchard Review* and Southern Illinois University Press, and the Crab Orchard Series in Poetry First Book Award contest screeners for making the publication of this book possible. Particular thanks to Brian Barker, contest judge, for choosing my manuscript.

"The Advance of the Glacier" was previously included in *The Laurel Review*. Thanks to Dana Levin for taking an interest in my work.

"The Succulent Flowers," "1900 Gibbon Street," and "The Age of Miracles" have appeared in *Blackbird*. Thanks to the editors and staff.

Finally, thanks to all my family, my friends, and my colleagues at Virginia Commonwealth University Libraries and throughout the university for their ongoing support.

PART ONE

The anthropologist asked the men if they ever
had visions. *We dream,* they said. Their dreams
had begun with his birth. His father had never
returned with the midwife, but after six hours,
had been found sprawled on the portico steps,
bound to the stones by his own frozen blood.

The anthropologist recalled his poor mother's
warning: *Your father left us for another woman. She
was cold and loved only the money.* For a time then,
his mother had taken in lodgers. The last had
beaten him senseless for opening the calfskin
notebook left on the divan in the music room.

The anthropologist touched his chest through
his jacket. Gunshots echoed in the hills, where
a hunting party had cautioned him not to stray
unattended. It was pheasant season. The fresh
snow had come up to their knees, and they all
had led him down a hidden road to the village.

These men had dreamed, too, of his mother's
screams when the lodger had broken the both
of her legs with the fire iron. Her son, not yet
nine years old, had held the unfamiliar, gloved
hand of a constable while the gathering crowd
watched the structure turn black and collapse.

Night had fallen long ago, so the men offered
the anthropologist a room in one of their very
finest homes. The bed had already been made
for him, and a hot bath was now being drawn.
They would leave him to himself for the night,
but would see him again when it was morning.

Plumes of smoke still rose from the exploded silos
on the outskirts. The ruins of the town smoldered.
Arion and his sister observed from the cliffs along
the perimeter of the garden on their estate. The air
in the house had grown close, she said. Her nerves
would soon break—for years now, Arion had been
giving her a pinch of arsenic in her nightly digestif.
The rapids below them choked with black timbers
and the bloating corpses of cattle. One look down
from the balustrade and the young woman fainted.
Her fall past the strata of recent times cut through
the carrion like a harrow. Her white skirt darkened.

Arion threw in after her the letters from her suitor,
Georg—that mere dealer in agricultural machines!
How often she had spoken of their shared passion
for science and the exhibition where they had first
met, the way their fingers had touched in reaching
to scrutinize the frond of a dwarf palm. Arion spat
the soot from his tongue. Men of the next century,
Georg had written, would cultivate crops sufficient
to stop hunger, hybrids that could cure disease and
even reveal light to blind eyes. Arion of course had
been born able to see for miles. Cinders shuddered
from the arms of the war cross in the town square.

In the forty-third dream, Sergeant at last was
allowed to trade wings of the house with his
brother, but Galbraith had left the windows
open through the recent storms. Frigate birds
were roosting in a wardrobe now overgrown
with lichens. As Sergeant grabbed their necks,
their hollow bones snapped, and the splinters
pierced his naked fingers. He wiped them on
an Easter dress that belonged to their sister,
Martha, who had gone missing only this year.

When Sergeant woke, it was half past seven.
Galbraith and Martha would have moved on
to the greenhouse to supervise the watering.
Sergeant would skip breakfast and go straight
to the study. He would say that he had been
awake since dawn and had lost track of time,
speculating on the future of glass architecture.
In theory, whole cities could be made of glass.
Glass walls, glass doors—even roofs of glass.
Citizens of glass cities would grow very close.

Sergeant dried his face beside the washbowl,
his burgundy nightshirt saturated with sweat.
Their father had always said, *Dreams can kill.*
Sergeant had heard him on the evening of his
death, from behind his locked chamber door,
speaking the name of their aunt—*Ermalinda.*
Martha said that dreams were pleasure cruises.
One met only nice people, and he conversed
or played games on deck—though sometimes
the ship sank, and he did not live to learn why.

Maurice knew now that he would die here, inside his grandfather's house. Then his body would lie in his grandfather's bed until the delivery service noticed last week's sausages rotting on the stoop. Not even the mission workers ever came to visit. What the residents of the suburb said was all lies, that his grandfather had employed unwholesome innovations—especially hypnotism—to compel his patients to love him and to do strange favors. Of course, such tales were not unlike the reek of smoke in the velvet drapes of the drawing room.

The bottles of chloroform in the basement had never been explained satisfactorily. Investigators had found dozens amidst the Edison recordings, trunks packed with suits cut in outdated fashion, and a human skeleton hanging in a vertical case. As a child, Maurice had never visited this house. His grandfather had always just sent cablegrams. He had told Maurice to give out his name, when abroad, to gain entrance to embassy functions— port and cigars among gentlemen conversing on world-record flights, new music, changing times.

On long evenings, Maurice liked to put on films from his grandfather's library and act out scenes from *Easy Virtue*, *The Cheat*, or *Flesh and the Devil* starring Greta Garbo. His favorite, in two parts, was *Dr. Mabuse, the Gambler*, in which the master mesmerist founded his empire on the science of manipulation. The countess could not persuade even his lover, the dancer, to betray him, despite the tightening of the dragnet. And while the end would always be the same, Cara would be lovely and dance every time Maurice restarted the film.

Dear shadow, I have wandered, sleepless,
down roads paved with gleaming ice, into
the hills of a strange county. Before me is
a walled estate. On the stone pillars hang
gates of iron. The lamps have not been lit
in years. Old snow piled up like sapphires
will not last. My older brother once tried
to hold his breath forever, and I continue
to dream that, in the brook, he rests, face-
down. The vest he wears is midnight blue.
Shadow, you offer nothing but the armor
plates of insects that you scoured clean in
a season not yet past us. My hands freeze.

The various fragments of the bathtub had
been reconfigured as a pyramid. The four
lion's feet lay at the corners. Mal watched
the dark water bubble up from the broken
pipe and wash across the tile floor, where
it lapped against the base of the pyramid.

He had been at the grocer's to buy tinned
mackerel—the insides of his icebox stank.
At the war memorial, the aged telegrapher
had stopped him to indicate a supernatural
sign, the gyrfalcon that soared in widening
circles above the fields of the Trask farm.

Mal placed his food on the kitchen table.
Until last week, he had owned a sideboard,
but it too had been ruined and assembled
pyramidally. He had discovered his china
stacked on the shelves within the icebox,
reeking of a thing from beyond the grave.

After that had come additional pyramids:
the pyramids of the bookcase, the leather
reclining chair, the medicine chest—even
the camphor trunk for the coats had been
obliterated. Smoke was in the air. Already
the townsfolk had begun burning leaves.

Mal swept up the remains of the bathtub
and dragged them out to the laurel hedge
separating his house from the north road
and the heath beyond. There he dug a pit
beside the five mounds of earth marking
the burials of the other, earlier pyramids.

Soon he would be sleeping on the floors
of an empty house, like a solitary badger
inside its hole. Before the snow, he ought
to pay the Trasks a visit. While they kept
to themselves, they had lived here longer
than anyone and knew the area inside out.

The council of the northern region led the man
sentenced to expulsion from the service of life
to the wall around the wilderness and stripped
him of his clothes, his spectacles, and, above all,
a pocket watch that had belonged to his father.
They opened the iron door of the Hare's Gate
and pushed him through before closing it once
again. The man screamed pleas for mercy, then
threats of return and vengeance. He continued
until his voice failed him. All had gone home.

The next morning, the man's wife and children
found the fruit in the dish blackened with flies.
By the end of the day, mold had covered every
loaf of bread from the bakery. The rivers were
dammed with dead salmon. When the sun rose
on the seventh day, the vultures had assembled
by the hundreds on top of the wall. They woke
the people with their chatter. The trees beyond
the wall had grown full and begun to bear fruit
as though the recent frosts had never occurred.

The council prescribed the slaughter of a hare.
The man's wife slit its throat and let the blood
drain on the dinner table. She removed its pelt
and laid it upon the seat of her husband's chair.
After the carcass had been burned, she ground
the bones in the fire and swept the warm ashes
into the bedclothes. She combed them through
her wet hair, then through that of the children.
As she stroked their curls with her ivory comb,
she instructed them both to bite their tongues.

The Quarantine

Aristotle would have to stay on the verandah
while his mother stepped out. *Let the catfish be,*
she said to him. *And don't touch that gramophone.*
He watched her disappear into the tall grasses
before he reached into the glass tank to chase
the catfish in circles. His hands brushed across
the alien scales and whiskers. He had read that
hurricanes threw sailors off ships. Their bodies
hung in the dark until the kraken caught them.

He went to the gramophone to play *Peer Gynt*.
Underneath the iron table, the ants had found
another dead crow. Soon there would be only
a skeleton. He had almost dozed off yesterday,
counting the insects collecting atop this or that
carcass lying about. His mother had been away
then, too—the usual visit to the Copley house.
He had never been there, but could just see it
from the attic window. It was near the church.

He had never been there either. Every Sunday,
the bells rang as always. *The poor chaplain won't
last more than a few weeks*, the boy's mother said.
Mrs. Copley used to drop in early on Sundays.
They had all sat upon the chairs in the garden,
around the statue of the Virgin. After prayers,
they had listened to *Peer Gynt*, and the women
had gazed off to the south road. *When Jedediah
was with us*, Mrs. Copley had said—never more.

One time, a tortoise had bitten the boy's finger. His mother had had to pry it off. *Someday, child, you'll find your head in the mouth of a puma.* He had tried to imagine that chamber of terrible silence, that black void. Were he a hero, he would force open the jaws with his bare hands and wrestle the creature down to the foot of the mountain where it would lie before him, tamed. The two would scour the country of villains and freaks.

He opened his eyes. He should not fall asleep. He should continue to survey the field beyond the barrier of salted earth. Still nothing moved at the trees on the road that passed the church, and the wooden gate remained closed. Nothing had ever appeared there but a single horse. His mother had shot it dead from a hundred paces, then covered it with branches and set it on fire. She had left its ashes and bones to the elements.

Mrs. Copley had stopped coming to the house around then. His mother had told him to keep alert whenever she paid calls. She had allowed the garden to go to seed—even the statue was streaked with bird droppings. *Peer Gynt* stayed in its sleeve. Day after day, he turned the pages of the same few illustrated books that showed heroes in confrontation with the spawn of hell, but every time he looked up, there was nothing.

The windows have turned white with the steam,
and still my sister asks for a stronger, hotter fire.
Her fever will soon have soaked the sheets with
corruption. *Why am I dying?* she says in the voice
of some insect. The migrating frogs on the road
are killed witlessly beneath the march of hooves
and jackboots. Crows pick through their entrails.

My sister's brow is like the snow. The only thing
to be done is to wait with her until death arrives.
Her bones ache, she tells me. The cup falls from
her hands and colors the sheets with weak broth.
I change them. Always a set of sheets boils while
another one dries in the wind. *Is it worth the effort?*
my sister once said. A crow lights at the window.

Nothing more will visit us before nightfall, when
my sister's eyes will close forever. I will continue
in this house. She never married. She never even
left the valley. But she leaves it now, as the frogs
migrate. The ones that fall in the road, split open,
have met a merciful end. Their pieces are carried
beyond the battles, to the crags shrouded in mist.

Sister, my lungs have never filled up with blood,
but I sit by you, sweating my life away. My hands
smear the words of a letter that I have addressed
to you, and all that I hear is that roaring fire. If I
could lie there for you, to fade like the smoke of
the cannons, would I choose to? Watch over me.
You must understand how much I resemble you.

PART TWO

Through the curtains in the foyer, he watched
the delivery van disappear behind the hedges,
as the first flurries of what would prove to be
a long winter blew into the yard. The printed
message on the side of the aluminum canister
read simply, *In remembrance.* He took the thing
inside and placed it on the credenza where he
kept nonfunctional keys. In the canister were
three varieties of artificially flavored popcorn
divided by wax-paper sleeves. Several kernels
spilled out into the dish of lavender potpourri.

When he answered the telephone, he strained
to hear a voice through the static disturbance.
Pardon? he said. Meanwhile, the skies had gone
dark. His aunt Mathilde had kept popcorn at
her vanity, in apothecary jars—blue popcorn
flavored, she had explained, with the essence
of violet. The foyer popcorn smelled vaguely
of urine. Never had his aunt taken the lid off
a jar to eat in his presence, seated among her
foreign fragrances. She had started every day
by pouring out the stale water from the lilies.

By morning, the streets of this remote suburb
would be impassable to motorcars. He would
go out walking and, in the vacant lot, give up
the popcorn to the elements. It would return
from the ice in spring, forgotten and without
color. His aunt Mathilde had recorded dates
in her private book. After her disappearance,
the inspectors had searched for it everywhere
and found only a set of envelopes containing
banknotes. A scattering of snow at the doors
to the balcony had suggested little to anyone.

Apollonius, father of five sons, had a simple life
in this valley until the night when the mob came
requiring his death. From the millrace, they had
pulled, that same hour, the inert, bloodless body
of the missing Darrow boy. The five sons were
obliged to bury their father, themselves, outside
the common cemetery. On his cross, townsfolk
leave putrefied meat even now. I never met him.

The men at the alehouse explained that the boy
had been found in seven pieces. I soon learned
the virtue of silence. As the sun sets, the chimes
of the campanile wake the migrating geese, and
the evergreens on the route out of town darken.
So starts my sixth year of living in the house of
a murderer. Where did the widow and her sons
go? The townsfolk tell me only, *Away from here.*

Often I dream that a strange man taps upon my
bedroom window. His are the skeletal hands of
my diseased father, and he asks if he might rest
beside me. My father died alone while I was off
traveling. Apollonius, would a man do to a boy
what they claim that you did? All of the children
shun this house, and they clear the streets every
morning when I visit the butcher's to get bacon.

The men who belonged to the mob, Apollonius,
were no older than your own children. The hair
on their faces was fresh—and surely invisible in
the glare of lanterns as they held you to the cold
floor and broke your ribs. They cut you open at
both the wrists and shoulders—everywhere that
you purportedly had done wrong. They left you
hanging on the notice board in the town square.

The chaplain watches from the vestry windows,
like the half-moon reflected on the millrace. He
tells me nothing, Apollonius, and still I beg him
to help me to turn back the shadows that linger
by my door at night. Believe, Apollonius, that I
will not be hanged just so that, once again, you
can die. I almost struck the boy whom I caught
scratching your name onto the gate, over mine.

If only my father had lived—if only I had never
moved out to this all-but-forgotten hell—things
here have been happening too long out of sight.
God, keep me apart from them. Make me a fog
on the millrace. Carry me off with the darkness.
The entire valley is chiseled from the same hard
stone. Barn owls strew the ground with feathers
while the rabbits impaled on their claws scream.

Nocturne (Craters of the Moon)

Dear shadow, for a long time I have lain
beside this window, afraid even to move,
and still the night must last hours longer,
hung from hooks of ice above the frozen
reservoir. Those blind fish are not biting.
I dreamed that my brother returned here
from his grave. *At dawn,* I said, *you will die
again. You ought to have stayed where you were,
under the snow.* He is, after all, a white fox
with green eyes that see into my dreams.
In the crook of my arm, he lies and rests
his teeth on my throat—as you, shadow,
wait by the door, with your bait and trap.

Once they had shared a bowl of onion stock,
Aldo and the schnauzer made their evening
pilgrimage. They stopped on the hill, outside
the ruined archway of what had been a friary,
and watched the motor van depart south, for
the city abattoir, from which it would return
empty and hosed clean. A distant, dim figure
pulled the steel gate shut. Only this past year
had Aldo given up his cataloguing the ancient
graffiti on the porphyry blocks strewn about.

The schnauzer put its nose down to the bare
soil under the cedar where, fifty years earlier,
the first of the wayfarers had been discovered
dead. Now he lay buried among many others,
beneath the obelisk erected for the unknown.
Aldo took the mouth harp from his pocket
and played the songs that he had heard sung
by field hands preparing the tractors at dawn.
The dog stood upon its hind legs and barked
in time. Soon the seasonal rains would begin.

Tomorrow, Aldo would wake yet again from
the dream in which his father returned home
from prison to bury him beneath the obelisk.
The schnauzer would stir at Aldo's cold feet,
as he slipped out of the bed to wash his face
at the basin full of wilting dahlias. And while
the glass paperweight would cast white flecks
of light into the gray alcove in which he had
spent another restless night, the blank, ruled
pages would remain fixed to his writing desk.

Mars would soon have the pleasure of confronting his manservant for giving him, every morning, this vitamin under false pretenses. Mars had kept exact measurements of his moustache, and not once had it grown by even a hair. The vitamin simply soured his stomach. He had considered attempting a dose higher, but he feared the possibility of a slow death.

Hardly three years had passed since his grandfather had gone to his eternal rest. What a moustache had grown on that face! All who had beheld it while he had lain in state had wished desperately to cut it off and wear it. After the room had emptied, Mars had walked back in to the coffin so that he might touch the preternaturally stiff bristles just one more time.

Of course, the other great moustache had belonged to the late Nietzsche. He had cultivated such a gem by means of an activity that he had termed *yes saying*, the undermining of those slavish morals darkening the actual world in favor of the supersensory realm of impossible Platonic ideals. It was mad to believe anything more real than a truly gigantic moustache.

By no account had Nietzsche been a man of virility. A brothel had had nothing to offer him but another opportunity to play the piano. In the days following his death, depraved people had stolen his moustache and held it for ransom, but there had been no buyers. The moustache had already become sublimated and taken the form of myth, timeless and without place.

Mars felt within himself a capacity for a moustache at least the size of his grandfather's. After breakfast, while annotating *Götzen-Dämmerung*, he reflected on the utopia of possessing a moustache that obscured one's face, like an executioner's mask. The *moment of the shortest shadow* drew near, when the errors of they who had thought Mars unworthy would be exposed.

Patiently, Mars looked forward to standing over his manservant and, while the cretin lay asleep, making a punitive, though decidedly heroic, use of the shears. The smirk that had been hidden there would vanish immediately. Shock and awe would contort his face as he saw on Mars a glorious moustache derived not from physical substance, but purely from the spirit.

Nietzsche would have had no need of this revenge against anyone so lowly. His own valet would have shrunk from contemplating growing even a pair of mere whiskers. And when, in the mornings, he had cleared the tray from his master's room, he would have made secretive, God-fearing bites at the sliver of burned crust, the last remains of the coffee cake.

Shortly before the Labrador's reappearance,
a team of traders had found Florian's uncle's
bicycle leaning unattended against the statue
of the lion on the eastern face of the bridge.
In these parts, it was said that any man who
threw himself from the bridge in the winter,
when the water at the bottom of the ravine
was frozen, would bring his dog back to life.

Along the fence, snags of fleece and a page
from the county paper flapped in the wind.
Florian looked to the bridge. Drays crossed
on the road to market, laden with the usual
wool. On the ground, the Labrador gnawed
at an old bootstrap. His uncle had told him
that the telegraphs could transmit messages
from one side of the continent to the other.

We saw nothing more, the traders had said. So,
they had heaved the bicycle up over the rail.
Then Florian had laid at the Labrador's feet
his uncle's dinner plate with a mutton chop
still steaming. The next morning, he had led
the dog through the empty village lanes and
around the prehistoric menhir, to the bluff,
to gaze down upon the white, solid cataract.

Now he was returning home from another
night's wandering, beside the upright posts
that cast regular shadows over the heather,
like the tracks of the railroad. His stomach
growled. The lion began turning golden in
the sun. Presently, he would meet the drays
in which the drivers sat smoking pipes and
laughing—none talking of the coming war.

Nocturne (Wind from the Hills)

Dear shadow, a cold lightning cracks
the sky, and the cloud of frozen dust
swells in the distance. I fill my hands
with steam, still waiting for someone
to appear from the west. My brother
never came with me into these fields.
Far from here he died, and he sleeps
as the wheat sleeps, in a bed of frost
polished like a mirror. Again the line
of black alders along the road begins
to move. You, shadow, leap the wall
and climb up the ladders of the silos.
Open wide their steel doors of night.

The Monster of Barlow

He hated this provincial village with the dairy
and its cheese that smelled of urine. He hated
the flies. He hated the hideous mongrel ducks
that excreted up and down the riverbanks. He
had implored the people thereabouts for work
carrying feed, mucking out stables—anything
to exhaust him so that he would not lie awake
beneath a mildewed thatch roof, in linens that
had been the property of some other lost soul.

They had refused him even work at the dairy.
Seldom did they condescend to speak to him.
He had given up hope. But every morning, he
received his parcel containing a cheese wedge
and miscellaneous defeathered parts of ducks.
He woke gasping and flung open his window.
The breeze smelled urinous. Flies came inside
and deposited their eggs on rags that covered
barely touched food left from the day before.

He pulled off the bedsheets and boiled them
in a rusting cauldron that turned them brown.
He dragged the straw mattress out to the yard
to beat it with a fire iron. He went to the river
to strip himself naked and enter the shallows,
where he would scrub his body with handfuls
of rocks. He bled. One time, the children had
taken his clothes and wiped dung upon them,
so he had threatened to poison the milk cans.

On the tenth anniversary of his political exile,
he shaved his head and gathered up the heap
in the leather pouch that had once contained
his favorite imported tobacco. He emptied it
into the river and watched the hair float away
toward the far capital. On the opposite bank,
a duck resting near a pool clogged with algae
appeared to vomit its meal, but choke it back.
He placed his head underwater and screamed.

Catching and strangling the ducks would not
be difficult. He could kill anything or anyone.
But the villagers wanted him to be a monster.
He had heard them saying to each other that
they had not worked so well together in years.
As he passed the dairy, two men shook hands
still covered with sweat from the cows' udders.
A bargain was struck. They shared duck jerky
and wiped the guts of flies onto their trousers.

The Diplomats

The daylight failed hours before. In the dark
alley, Sam Curwen slips on the cobblestones
while he does the last of his trouser buttons.
Shards of ice pierce his bare palms. He takes
up his deerstalker and shakes it off, the odor
of his late stepfather's sweat rising like moths.
He dries himself with a handful of unspoiled
snow from the ledge of a shuttered window.

The three gentlemen standing at the mouth
of the alley, beneath the gas lamp, each wear
the same black overcoat and derby. The one
on the left turns up a wristwatch. *The regent,*
he says, *will have made his decision.* The others
say, *Death.* They all move out of sight, down
Greville Street, where the carriages wait for
the correct fare. In the frigid wind, Curwen
puts his bloody hands back into his pockets.

He will continue to cross the narrow district
on the long way home from the locksmith's.
Business is slow. Around here, many homes
have been shut up for winter. And the snow
may start again tonight—already the seventh
time this month. The two horses that died in
Jake Hom's shed were hauled on oilskins out
into the street. The bonfire left a black pool.

The monster Leviathan spiraled about the ivory handle of the reading glass, with treasure ships trapped in its jaws. The book of sagas lay open atop the count's table. He ate oranges, plucking the seeds from his mouth, like coins. This year's crop nearly toppled the trees brought out from the orangery. He even gave fruit to his servants to flavor their otherwise-bland evening custard.

Since the outbreak of war, he had had months to himself to continue his study of the ancient chieftains who had built chapels decorated with skulls of invaders—blood had been their paint. The count arranged the last seed atop the heap of skins on his tray. Gunfire down in the valley once more brought to mind the fruit dropping to the gravel lanes of his symmetrical gardens.

The last reports from neighboring landowners had been of the highway closures, trade delays, and the imminent cease of couriers. The count recalled a sentence from one missive especially. Arion of Oster had foretold his sister's demise: *Her trembling hands have become little more than glass ornaments.* She would not outlast this war. How many others would die by the merciless sword?

The Palace of the West Wind had been looted and burned. The count's nearest cousin, killed in flight to their ancestral lodge. The portraits, the archive of correspondence: these were lost forever. And yet, jewels, gold, and silver could be recovered. A new palace could be founded upon the ruins of the old. The count lay awake into the night fragrant with oranges, dreaming.

PART THREE

In the back room of his shop, the butcher cleaves
the last of the morning's carcasses. The dawn has
passed. In the mews, the child cannot scream, for
the procurer's hand covers her mouth. Tonight is
the sacrificial augury. The goat god will rise again
and breathe into his listeners' ears. The bell rings
at the shop front, where the servant girls browse
hung rabbits and plates of hogsheads and trotters.
The butcher wraps their lamb chops in the heavy
waxed paper. The girls have come from the East
for work serving good households. Daily, they do
the shopping, wash the clothes and floors, empty
and scour the chamber pots—their lives are built
on filth. To the butcher, they might as well come
from the top of the world, the frozen wilderness
where fools go seeking gold and monsters' tusks.
He would cut off both of his thumbs rather than
go there. All the people of the East are cold, and
their god is nothing but smoke and chiseled stone.
Before the open back window, the plucked wings
and breasts from seventeen geese glisten with fat,
gray and purple viscera beside them, in the bowl.

Years ago, on the same terrace, Thor's aunt Hilde
had brought him a roast-beef sandwich. For hours,
he had reclined there, beneath the woolen blanket,
while the wind had whistled through the balustrade.
He had already grown used to wearing dark glasses,
so he had watched the line of his fellow guests and
bathers taking the path to the stairs down the cliff.

Their voices had disappeared into the endless surf.
Beside Thor, Hilde had busied herself with another
provocative memoir that she would not read aloud.
The surf is enough for you. The bathers had carried out
umbrellas and insulated flasks of fortifying mineral
water—details with which Thor had formed an idea
of the afterlife. *Won't they be overwhelmed by the current?*

He had waited all day to see them return: the niece
of a baron who had willed her nothing, the former
athlete, the scholar of dead languages—despite his
weak eyes, Thor had come to recognize everybody
over the months of monotony. He had finished his
sandwich, even the white lace of fat that Hilde had
refused to trim. *What doesn't kill us makes us stronger.*

Hilde had grown old before her time. Never again
would she have sufficient strength to wrap a shawl
around her own shoulders as she sat on the terrace.
From the door of the doctor's suite, Thor watched
a nurse help her to eat clear broth. *You're doing fine.*
The doctor emptied his pipe, and the embers faded,
a phantom in the glass ashtray beside the diagnosis.

Thor had never found the remains of a tern among the sea wrack and driftwood. Perhaps the birds fell far from land and were swallowed up by the abyss. After lunch, he would descend to the vacant beach where, the week before his twenty-ninth birthday, he had come upon the impression of an enormous ammonite on an outcrop that had since collapsed.

Only the first few guests had arrived. This evening, the vocalist would perform in the salon. *A new piece by Nielsen.* Thor would provide the accompaniment on piano, while the pair of business travelers from the continent would stand at the window hung with silk drapes, blowing cigar smoke from their nostrils like dragons. *Do you recommend the bathing? As always.*

Nocturne (Empty Fireplace)

Dear shadow, last week's rack of lamb
rots on the dinner table, while the flies
lay eggs that will soon blister apart like
a sickness. The air is heavy with vapor.
The beams of the roof hang overhead
on their swollen joints. At the window,
my dead brother watches me. *A dream*,
I tell myself, but I turn toward the pail
and vomit. The scent of corrosion fills
my nostrils, as I lift my skull and listen
for the faint stirring of the boreworms.
Shadow, how long will you lean there,
holding the damp cloth and whistling?

Norbert was wont to blame the nosebleeds, too, on
his continuing discord with a neighbor in a parallel
world—in this house, the boundary between planes
thinned almost to transparency. Norbert's first day
upon moving here had ended with his blacking out
in the bath, and since then, headaches, nausea, and
such ills had been making him into a regular invalid.

His chief duty, therefore, was to gauge the capacity
of the house for serving a malign will. He devoted
countless hours to scrutinizing the pastoral scenes
printed on the wallpaper in the sitting room, for he
had a recurring dream in which he discovered the
carpet strewn with offal from a recently butchered
elk. When he woke, the air smelled stale and gamy.

On account of the cold drafts that the repairmen
could never locate, he often became fevered, even
delirious. In the sitting room, he watched the light
from the setting sun through the glass front door
burn onto the wall a red portal. His physician had
diagnosed a case of nerves and prescribed strong
tranquilizers—yet what protection were dull wits?

Everything in this world corresponded to, or was
inhabited by, something from another—the door
had its shadow door; the sun had its shadow sun.
And what might seem a whimsical circuit through
this suburb, made by Mrs. Loden with her beagle
on their evening walk, was in reality the signature
of an alien intelligence laboring for some purpose.

Indeed, was Mrs. Loden human at all? Could it be that she and the beast together were but an image of a hungering nothing, vacuous and weightless as its very concept? Norbert pulled his muffler tight. How best was he to guard himself? Were he ever to leave this house, his tribulations might cease— or might he himself as easily vanish into oblivion?

Or wherever he went in this world, might he find the same wallpapered room and the same chimera of woman and dog making its paranormal patrol? In a remote village of the Klondike, with a winter sun that never rose and struck his garret window, he would be no safer. Miners one after the other disappeared into an unmapped, frozen wilderness.

He would stay where he happened to be, reading Hegel's unfolding of the history of all-consuming *Geist* through its phenomenological moments of body and mind, servitude and liberty. Something existed so that nothing might also, and vice versa. Between the something and the nothing lay their mutual necessity, a force forever becoming aware.

In the Forest of Moär beyond the Trask farm
stood a pyramid of red stones. *Old as the land,*
some said. Others said that druids had built it
and had gone feral—shunning language, even
clothing. They had eaten meat off the carcass.

No one in town had actually seen the pyramid.
Indeed, a few said that it did not exist—except
in the dreams of those careless wanderers who
approached the forest, or those who, at night,
fell asleep before having closed their windows.

Not a word of this to the children, they all insisted.
On his morning walks, Mal talked to the men
who smoked their pipes by the war memorial.
They recounted stories of their ancestors who
had caught fire merely by looking at the forest.

Once, a hot wind had blown from the north,
over Moär, bearing the reek of burning flesh.
At least two dozen folk that day had suffered
pains in the stomach or issues of blood from
the mouth. None had ever recovered entirely.

Another time, Uriah Hellman, the invalid, had
been seen two places at once: in his chamber,
reading aloud passages from the Good Book,
and more than a mile away, pouring kerosene
in a triangle around Lionel Matheson's house.

The men said that the age of miracles had not
ended. Three Trask boys had come into town
the same day that Mal had taken up residence.
No one had known them, but like every Trask
they had worn on their feet only wraps of skin.

Mal took to shutting his windows at nightfall.
Before bed he lit the lamps in the living room
and started the Victrola—records of hit songs.
But lamps went out before dawn, and records
lasted only so long, music giving way to a hiss.

The Marshes

Fifty-six years after the plague of frogs,
the villagers continued to find skeletons
inside tinder boxes and barrels of wine,
beneath their hearthstones, and behind
religious icons. At one time, the ground
had been carpeted in the tiny carcasses.
The villagers crushed the dried remains
into a powder for alleviating conditions
of the lungs. Moisture in the air turned
all their eaves and shutters slowly black.
The carpenter, with his remaining sons,
took payments in pulverized skeletons.

Families who ran short of their powder
tried to replicate it using fish skeletons,
fossil shells, dried silt—even the bones
of persons who had perished drowning
in their own mucus. But ingesting these
typically ended in death. Each summer,
the children went back to the waterway
to go swimming. They staged contests:
who could find hidden treasure or hold
his breath the longest. The littlest ones
folded paper boats and watched as they
sank, floating south toward the marshes.

Nocturne (Boat at the Wayside)

Dear shadow, I am not alone even now
on the abandoned towpath. The moon,
broken into pieces, floats on the brook,
as a night wind shakes free the tangled,
dry reeds of last year. My breath echoes
and dissolves like fog. Should I lie here,
with the broken moon, or would I only
climb out of this cold water, shivering?
My brother entered the brook long ago,
and his mouth was covered with hands
of ice. Shadow, you sprawl on the bank
and say nothing. Where did the insects
that sang during summer go? They died.

The habitants of Lesser Ransom, long acquainted with evil, looked up from their preparations for the difficult winter. The elder explained, *The Prince of Darkness comes riding his chariot.* Of course, the experimental balloonist heard precious little over the roaring fire that kept him aloft in the heavens. Instead, he observed the villagers' kneeling as one in prayer. Perhaps he thought that they praised almighty God for the miracle of manned flight.

All around them were strewn their antique implements: their reapers, their knives for slaughter—and on the air, a tang of guts, pigs' insides suspended from iron hooks that turned in the wind. The balloonist took off his cap and waved to the villagers, who could make nothing of the letters in gold on the side of his basket. They knew simply that from the earth, this infernal thing had risen and that to the earth, it must return via a burning door.

Whatever the balloonist may have said then, as he fell, no one understood. He became lost within the brilliant folds of wreckage crowning a nearby hill. The villagers crossed themselves. And when the machine had finally grown cool, they heaped stones atop it—like, they said, the monuments once built by their heathen forefathers when terrible kings and warlords had been summoned to the halls of the death god in his mantle of white fur.

The sheep bucked on its tether, about its neck
a collar of blood. From the barn, I had hauled
out the cart for the long ride to market. I only
stood there, watching as the creature smashed
the water trough with its skull, its teeth falling
into the trampled straw. Of course, the tether
broke. I had never learned how to stop it. But
the men at market would laugh. *You have a gift
for losing things, Ludo. You should try counting them.*

I chased the sheep down the empty macadam,
praying, *God, make it slip. Make it collapse from a
concussion.* Instead, it burned with a kind of fire,
bright flames streaming through its coat. I too
burned with a fire that stripped the flesh from
my ribs. But I came no closer to catching that
runaway sheep—as I could not have saved my
own brother from the conflagration years ago.
The sheep totally vanished into the cornfields.

The stalks bent over me, and in the cold mud,
I lost the trail of blood. At the irrigation ditch,
the fog that had been gathering since morning
descended upon me. If the owner of this field
discovered the sheep, he would lead it, bound,
to the other men. *What have you done to it?* they
would say. *A wife would be less grief.* They would
bring back the sheep, with its ear tag polished
like a wedding ring, a red ribbon on its throat.

So, I would have to kill the sheep, myself, and
sell the meat. My brother had done the killing,
before I had killed him by overturning a lamp
in the old hayloft. Next market, I would bring
a new sheep, and still the men would say, *How
good to see the both of you again.* They would open
the sheep's mouth and touch the perfect teeth.
It's a miracle! they would say. *You've made it well.
You must treat it as you do your own flesh and blood.*

God, I said, *keep this sheep out of the hands of men
forever. And keep me, although I should be punished.*
Around me, the fog tightened. I saw nothing
ahead, but I heard then the same faint ringing
in my ears that I had in the tin shed just after
a slaughter. I prayed that, in its shroud of fog,
the sheep would reach the south moor, where
the foxes and the vultures would find it. They
asked nothing and did not return a lost sheep.

Albrecht slipped one last visiting card under
the locked door of what he seemed to recall
being the oriental-damask salon. Mort must
encounter it eventually. There on the trefoil
end table, across from the grandfather clock
that rang the hour, Mort's pet monkey fixed
its eyes upon Albrecht. The dying sun drew
the gray shadows of the urns on the terrace
up the west wing and into a portrait gallery
where the painted faces of past generations
had, over time, bleached almost to nothing.

Albrecht had left Mort to tend to the house
while he had been taking his rest at the lakes
after their mother had passed away violently.
When he had come back, able to walk again
with the aid of his cane, he had found most
of the rooms locked. Their drapes had been
closed, and around the doors hung the faint
fragrance of camphor. Through the keyhole
of their mother's chamber, he had glimpsed
the specters of her lamp and the méridienne
from which she had habitually read the tarot.

The monkey had followed Albrecht as far as
the artificial ruins at the edge of the grounds
while he wandered in search of his vanished
brother. Some nights, a figure had emerged
from one of those locked rooms and spread
white sheets on the lawn, to lay out all sorts
of bric-a-brac. From his bedroom windows,
Albrecht had attempted to recognize objects
that he had not seen in many years. The box
for envelopes with a matching silver blotter
had caused him often to lie awake worrying.

Albrecht had once heard the peacock's call,
and the memory of a green china doorknob
had surfaced. After scouring every corridor,
he had given up. He had taken to hobbling
down the road in recent days, to the tavern
where no one had recognized him, to enjoy
several songs with the anglers. He had gone
with them in their boats and seen the mists
dissolve in the morning light. Which is why
right now a car waited in the porte cochere.
The merchant liner would be leaving today.

PART FOUR

The rot of flesh nested in every corner of the house.
All fifty-five rooms had been tainted. Arion smelled
it on his hands even after a hot bath. He had turned
away homeless townsfolk coming to his door all day.
My sister was killed, he had said. *Soldiers came ransacking.*
Of course, soldiers had not come this way. His sister
lay where she had fallen, at the bottom of the gorge,
with the debris and corpses lodged among the rocks.

The lower half of one man's face had been blistered
from burns. His swollen hands, bound in torn strips
of muslin. His bride had not wept. Beneath her eyes
had been the bruises of nights lived in mortal fear—
Arion now realized the uncanny likeness to his sister
in her last few days. That pair of beggars had walked
away from the house and down the avenue of limes,
like two nags loaded with spent coals from the boiler.

Only a few of the servants remained. Most had fled
when the valley had been set on fire. Arion assumed
them all dead. He might have employed the beggars
had they been rather more intact and had references.
In the kitchen, the cook cut a pheasant into morsels
for stew. Simple food like this would have to suffice
until the rebel provinces had admitted defeat, which
could not be much longer—winter was approaching.

Arion looked at his sister's empty place over supper.
She had tapped her fork upon the charger whenever
she had felt unable to eat. Before dark, Arion would
go out to the terrace that overhung the gorge, to see
if vultures had plucked out her eyes. He would have
much to tell the count, the closest of his confidants,
by the time the postal couriers resumed. In the long
salon, the gilt pendulum of the clock slivered the air.

Killy was still contemplating his tiles. Ephraim had waited three hours, watching the shadows of icicles lengthen across the patterned carpet. With a five of bamboo, he would win, be done with this awful game. Clyde unwrapped a fresh piece of flavored chewing gum. Since Tuesday, he not taken nourishment. He would continue only to weaken as they all did—all but Kaspar. From the wheel of white cheese, Killy carved one almost transparent sliver. Back and forth on the waxed marquetry table paced Kaspar's parrot. Ephraim wanted its neck in his hands.

In the magnificent days of antiquity, retainers had made no practice of mummifying parrots to accompany their pharaohs into the afterlife. Rather, they had mummified cats. Concealed beneath the feathers of a bird was a skeleton, while shaving a cat's hair left a cat. Ephraim's had licked itself bald through the drab nights. Now the parrot raked its black tongue across an empty gum wrapper exuding the fragrance of artificial orange. Kaspar gave his bird some boiled chicken. *That turns my stomach*, said Killy. *Win the game*, said Kaspar, *and you'll be feeding it*.

Killy was wagering his lucky dog. Of course,
his lucky rabbit had brought no luck last year.
If Kaspar won, then he would collect the dog
and stuff it just as he had the rabbit, as he had
Ephraim's gopher, Clyde's frogs—everything
that the three had wagered. They always lost,
and he had lined up his inert trophies around
the room as though it were a tomb. This year,
Ephraim was wagering his cat. There simply
was nothing left—no carp, no bats. Not even
the rat traps in the cellar had yielded anything.
He found it harder and harder to make a catch.

At last Killy discarded. Ephraim could discard
a spring tile that got him nowhere. He prayed
and came up with only another useless season:
winter. The parrot, which had been mutilating
one edge of the score sheet, turned over a tile:
the five of bamboo. Undoubtedly, the bird was
clairvoyant. Killy believed the same of his dog.
At every touch of its nose on his bare ankles,
he stared as though toward his future triumph,
the winning hand. Ephraim had often seen him
blindfold the dog and lay out four faded prints.
It had unfailingly chosen *The Garden of Paradise*.

At one time, Killy had owned two myna birds that had known how to speak. Clyde's toucan had loved to catch balls. Ephraim had trained his macaw to play dead whenever Kaspar had so much as looked at it. But none of the birds had shown even the least interest in mahjong, and now they were lost, staring with glass eyes from their different corners of the game room, which had formerly housed the family records. Ephraim looked out the windows at the park, empty, white, and free of footprints. The snow crowning the marble obelisk fell to the ground.

Every night, Ephraim read alone in his room accounts of the polar expeditions—icebreakers that had frozen in place and been abandoned, the ceaseless night, the crews consuming dogs bred to die in the harness for the great cause: science. Ephraim took out his tobacco pouch. Shipmates offered each other their own bodies as food and were refused. But days later began the tearing of hair, the fighting among the sick over who had strength, who should be killed first. Kaspar discarded his tile and drew again. *The devil take it!* he said. *I'm still only one tile short.*

Every time Leighton wore the crocodile mask
out into the center of the lake, his chief desire
was to scream. Instead, he opened the ceramic
urn and spread the remains handful by handful
until there was nothing left for him. Today, he
conducted the burial of the late village cooper.

Disrespect had brought him shame. He wore
on his back the indelible stripes of his father's
chastening him for vomiting on the lakeshore.
The night of that sad episode, his mother had
prayed to the lake that she have years enough
to see her boy bring up a son who was better.

His father had died while asleep, and at dawn,
his mother had stripped the bed of the linens
and commissioned the pyre builder. Leighton
had gathered the ashes, still warm, for his first
burial. On the water, they had turned to a gray
scum oscillating back and forth on the ripples.

His mother had begun to invite young girls to
their home for him to court. Over sweet milk
and cakes, each one admired the family china,
portraits of past crocodiles, and those skeletal
shapes of frost on the windowpanes—asking
at last to see the mask and press her lips to it.

The cooper's son had told Leighton that two
girls had fought over him. Adriane Sturridge's
face was bruised and covered with bite marks
that had come to be gruesomely infected, and
the doctor had been forced to shave her head.
She had twice now tried to take her own life.

The cooper's son too was a bachelor, but had suffered many rejected proposals of marriage. He implored Leighton to take a wife soon, or no beautiful girls would remain in the village. Everybody would respect Leighton's decision regardless. The word of the crocodile was law.

The Wall

At the last lodge, the men said to follow the wall
along the edge of the moor until finally it opened
onto the old road leading north. But hours since,
this moor has swallowed the world. The leagues
of scrub grass, bent by the wind of the new year,
arrive at nothing. The men laughed when I said
that my own ancestors had erected the wall, that
most had disappeared into the hills, and not one
had come out for more than two hundred years.
In several places now, the wall has been broken,
letting me see the opposite side—to the horizon,
another moor. There was a tree once, miles away,
and I watched its limbs rake across the blank sky.

The ice under my feet whitens like a fog. Have I
taken the wrong way? Has no one come this far
in living memory? If I continue for much longer,
my heart will be just another stone block among
the fragments, and who then will say to the men
at the lodge that they lied to me? The hearth fire
licks the soles of their boots while they fill their
bellies with good ale and boiled brisket. I shared
stories of my forefathers, chieftains who crossed
the sea at the northernmost peninsula in winter.
They returned speaking of ice plains and whales
that swallowed ships whole. Theirs sons marked
their graves with cairns that would last millennia.

I have begged the wall to open, to acknowledge
in me my ancestors. I have begged for a traveler
to meet me and say, *Better awaits*—or, *Turn back.*
That way leads to the cliffs, where ancient boulders fall
to the straights that only the dead could hope to navigate.
But no traveler comes. The wall does not open.
The kestrels dive and pluck young rabbits from
their invisibility—my ancestors hide themselves
like this, I tell myself. I simply cannot see them.
But no—I have a wall. What I want are legends.

The Sluice Gate

The pelicans had come again to the village,
so the people abandoned work in the fields
of blighted wheat to collect their heirlooms.
They gathered by the canal, where the birds
were resting. For hours, the people watched
while thunderheads darkened their rooftops,
their calloused fingers worrying the familiar
contours of stone idols turned up by plows.

At the supper hour, the pelicans swallowed
a few of the offerings and took off in flight.
Households with nothing left would thrive.
The others collected white feathers to bind
to their remaining objects. They would seal
these amulets in the bottom compartments
of the cedar chests in which they kept their
heaviest coats, to wait out the next century.

Already Pendragon's bones had turned black
in the furnace. Winchester, sound asleep, had
licked the scales of blood off of his forearms.
I lay sprawled beside him, with the six others,
on the hot stones around the open iron door.

They too had closed their eyes, and dreamed,
I supposed, of the shore—a summer holiday
that would not come. Upstairs, the windows
had all frozen over, and now gave off a glow
blue and cold like the sea beneath an iceberg.

Back when there had been twenty-five of us,
we had huddled together in a common room,
praying for the sun to reappear. Then one day,
Dean Ives had tried to reach the Silex building,
where the chimneys had ceased issuing smoke.

Soon we had finished off the food, and death
had found Mowbray, who had torn the pages
from his diaries and swallowed them, leaving
us to divvy him up twenty-three ways equally.
We had begun counting survivors, not weeks.

Eventually, Cy Cromlech, the heartiest fellow,
had braved the wasteland of the second floor
in order to peer out, yet even he had returned
with frostbitten fingers and his face bloodless.
No sign, he had said, that there had been life.

Did the earth move, or had it too frozen over
like some prehistoric organism in amber? We
no longer spoke, but we listened as the bones
and broken furniture, the paintings and books
settled into the heap of ashes. Little remained.

Whenever a coal fell from the furnace, we all
fought for it. Perhaps each of us longed to be
the last one alive. I dreamed of going feet first
through the burning door. There I would find
a fire and, above all, the pain, the eternal pain.

In the forty-second dream, Sergeant was out
on the water, punting in their father's empty
casket. Galbraith called again from the shore,
where a desert wind stirred the grave clothes.
We must return the body to its eternal rest, he said.
Behind the iron gate, the dogs watched, with
the cloudy, putrescent saliva suspended from
their lips. Sergeant only began to recite verse,
as Galbraith took up in his arms what he saw
was little more than a mummified crocodile.

Even after he woke, Galbraith's nostrils were
filled with the ripe smell of coagulated blood.
Morning was far off. He opened the window
and looked beyond the high gate to the shore
of the lake that their father had ordered dug.
Below, a flickering light from the glass doors
onto the terrace revealed among the shadows
their sister, Martha, in her shawl of lilac crêpe
de chine, inspecting the leaves of the animal
topiaries. Sergeant's curtains were still drawn.

Every morning at breakfast, Martha offered
the chair on her right to Sergeant. Galbraith
had always wanted it. Across from her stood
their father's empty seat, upon which Martha
set the painted porcelain figurine of a hunter
with a pack of hounds lying at his feet. *How I
like to remember him,* she said. Their father had
covered the walls with the taxidermied heads
of elk. In the glass spheres replacing the eyes,
Galbraith traveled from one door to another.

Tomorrow, I can remove these bandages and hold things again with my left hand. The saw has lain in the field, where I dropped it, since it caught my knuckles. Only a fraction of that damned fence had been completed. With my one good hand, I stretched copper wire from the hill to the battle marker on the road west. I pulled up briars by the roots with this hand and planted them in the Derringers' pastures.

If anything but the Derringers' cows noticed, I would be surprised. The animals just stood on the opposite side of the wire and stared at my nine acres that they had been in the habit of trampling. *Our grandfather,* Keith Derringer had told me, *cleared this land when he settled here. If you want a fence, you build it, yourself.* I climbed the hill at night and looked down on them in that ugly stone house with its many additions.

After my hand filled up with pus, I drained it and dressed it with iodine. The yellow fingers left their grisly print on a leaf of blotter paper, so I carried it, under cover of darkness, out to the Derringers' barn and nailed it to the door. The gabled roof high above me drove a black wedge into the sky, and the clouds broke. My hex, my proclamation of war, dissolved, and I ran home, cradling my hand like a sick lamb.

I prayed that lightning obliterate the barn and
everything that the Derringers had. *Ruin them!*
I prayed. *Even if my own farm stays barren forever,
ruin them.* In the morning, I found the wires of
the fence stripped back and welded into a fist.
The way between farms was open, and already
the legion had gathered itself upon the hilltop.
I would tell anyone who asked at market how
it had happened, what I had done to my hand.

Every night in these barracks, the miners dream
of breaking through the granite walls of another
black tunnel, expecting to find there a chamber
of pure gold. Calder drops the canary in its cage,
and they watch the color fade. When they wake,
they gather at the narrow tables of the mess hall
and push dead weevils around in their rice gruel.
The morning will still be dark for several hours.
Calder says, *Forgive me.* Some touch his shoulder
while all of them return their bowls to the cook.

On duty, they give the bird their biscuit crumbs,
trembling as, stone after stone, tunnels lengthen.
Whenever they grow faint, they close their eyes,
and the flames that light up their carbide lamps
paint the undersides of their eyelids pale yellow.
Darach died in the collapse nearly six years ago.
He had spoken about how his mother had worn
a mask to hide her disfiguration. Before the last
time she had gone selling her handmade gloves,
she had kissed him once on the top of his head.

Then Henley said that he would leave the mine
for the charterhouse, to take vows as a brother.
When will you come back to us? Burwell asked him.
Henley said, *The monastery walls forever circumscribe
God's world.* Rupert began to cry, but said simply
that he thought of Darach laid out on the floor,
with his arm stretched from under the boulders
and to his pickaxe beside the extinguished lamp.
On that day, as on every other day, their voices
vanished down the branches of a long network.

Nocturne (Tremors of the Earth)

Dear shadow, electric lights burn once more
throughout this remote valley, though night
arrived hours ago. Darkness will be restored
shortly. My only photograph of my brother
fell from the bedroom mantel and woke me
from the dream in which I visited his grave.
I always wanted to believe that the dead lay
in undisturbed sleep. You, shadow, become
still, listening to the footsteps and blunders
of the fearful who retire one after the other
in their homes above you. In the plane tree,
the owl straightens its feathers, compacting
its prey into a sphere of bone and gray hair.

Galen lifted his glass to his brother's—a toast
to their father, who turned sixty that day. And
yet his glass touched nothing. His brother was
not there. Nor were his father and his beloved
hounds, Alfons and Karl. The table was empty.

In a tureen emblazoned with the family's crest,
the sauce for the hare pie had congealed. Galen
had been alone for seventeen years. The rest of
the hunting party had died in the avalanche and
now lay buried beneath the collapsed mountain.

Therefore, Galen burned the house and stables,
and the rotting timbers turned to white smoke.
He took a room in the village before Silas Pass,
above the shop dealing in secondhand clothing
and miscellaneous junk. His life became simple.

Out of scraps, he made toy animals. The trunk
in the shop window was crammed with badgers
foxes, and bears. Of these, he had kept a single
badger for himself, but it had spawned dreams
in which he had stitched it over his right hand.

When he woke, the first real snow for the year
had already fallen. His stove had gone out early
in the night, and once he had sat up, his breath
emerged pale, symptomatic of a lingering fever.
Ahead of him was a morning of the usual work.

Through the streets, the children had left their
footprints in knots from chasing each other as
they played at being the slayers of trolls, beasts
made wholly of blue ice, that would, according
to legend, someday return to the world of men.

Had Galen ever had an older brother who had called him outside in his coat, to heat the water for the horses? The horses' nostrils had glazed with mucus as somebody, perhaps his brother, had told him, *Everything will be yours when I leave.*

Had Galen ever had a father to promise to take him shooting once he had grown old enough to carry and aim a gun? He had seen trophy heads hung on the wall of a smoking room someplace and shaken the soot from a bearskin hearth rug.

But here in this room, there was no bear's skin, and the village children, who built fortifications and castles out of snow, had their own brothers. Galen splashed his face with water and felt as if he had just been slapped. Its sting faded slowly.

If Galen had ever dreamed something else, then he must have forgotten it while picking through sacks from the traders, full of breeches or shirts stained with food or wine. He held up the ruddy silk lining of a jacket to a fox's unfinished paws.

NOTES

"The Lost Psychotherapist": The movies referred to are Alfred Hitchcock's *Easy Virtue* (1928), Cecil B. DeMille's *The Cheat* (1915), Clarence Brown's *Flesh and the Devil* (1926), and Fritz Lang's *Dr. Mabuse, der Spieler* (1922).

"The Order of Silence": With particular respect to Shūji Terayama's movie *Saraba Hakobune* (1984).

"The Quarantine": The work referenced is Edvard Grieg's suite *Peer Gynt*, op. 23 (1876).

"The Passing Brigade": With particular respect to Kenji Miyazawa's poem "Matsu no Hari" (1922), translated as "Pine Needles" by Hiroaki Sato.

"The Blizzard": With particular respect to the Cyberdreams computer game *Dark Seed* (1992).

"The Burial Plot": With particular respect to James Wright's poem "At the Executed Murderer's Grave" (1958).

"The Hour of Study; or, The Concept of Moral Genealogy": The principal work referenced is Friedrich Wilhelm Nietzsche's book *Götzen-Dämmerung, oder, Wie man mit dem Hammer philosophiert* (1889), translated as *Twilight of the Idols, or, How to Philosophize with a Hammer* by R. J. Hollingdale.

"Hotel Vitruvius": With particular respect to Marcel Proust's novel *À la recherche du temps perdu* (1913–27), translated as *Remembrance of Things Past* by C. K. Scott Moncrieff and Terence Kilmartin.

"1900 Gibbon Street": The work referenced is Georg Wilhelm Friedrich Hegel's book *Phänomenologie des Geistes* (1807), translated as *Phenomenology of Spirit* by A. V. Miller.

"The Fog": With particular respect to William Everson's poem "The Screed of the Frost" (1949).

"The Years Underground": With particular respect to Sōseki Natsume's novel *Kōfu* (1908), translated as *The Miner* by Jay Rubin.

Muse
Susan Aizenberg

Millennial Teeth
Dan Albergotti

Lizzie Borden in Love:
Poems in Women's Voices
Julianna Baggott

This Country of Mothers
Julianna Baggott

The Black Ocean
Brian Barker

The Sphere of Birds
Ciaran Berry

White Summer
Joelle Biele

Rookery
Traci Brimhall

USA-1000
Sass Brown

In Search of the Great Dead
Richard Cecil

Twenty First Century Blues
Richard Cecil

Circle
Victoria Chang

Errata
Lisa Fay Coutley

Salt Moon
Noel Crook

Consolation Miracle
Chad Davidson

From the Fire Hills
Chad Davidson

The Last Predicta
Chad Davidson

Furious Lullaby
Oliver de la Paz

Names above Houses
Oliver de la Paz

The Star-Spangled Banner
Denise Duhamel

Smith Blue
Camille T. Dungy

Seam
Tarfia Faizullah

Beautiful Trouble
Amy Fleury

Sympathetic Magic
Amy Fleury

Soluble Fish
Mary Jo Firth Gillett

Pelican Tracks
Elton Glaser

Winter Amnesties
Elton Glaser

Strange Land
Todd Hearon

Always Danger
David Hernandez

Heavenly Bodies
Cynthia Huntington